NOAH AND THE ARK

Publishers Since 1798

THOMAS NELSON PUBLISHERS
Nashville

First published in 1993 by
Thomas Nelson Publishers, Nashville, Tennessee.

Story retold by Bill Yenne

Edited by Lynne Piade. Art and design direction by Bill
Yenne. Illustrated by Pete Avdoulos, Mark Busacca, Emi
Fukawa, Victor Lee, Wendy K. Lee, Douglas Scott, Peggy
Smith, Alexandr Stolin, Vadim Vahrameev, Hanako
Wakiyama, Nelson Wang and Bill Yenne.

Produced by
Bluewood Books (A Division of The Siyeh Group, Inc.)
P.O. Box 460313, San Francisco, CA 94146

Noah and the Ark.
    p.   cm. — (Children's Bible Classics)
    Summary: A simple retelling of the Bible story in which
Noah uses an ark to save himself and his family from a
worldwide flood.
    ISBN 0-8407-4914-7 (TR)
    ISBN 0-8407-4910-4 (MM)
    1. Noah's ark—Juvenile literature.   2. Noah (Biblical
figure)—Juvenile literature.   3. Bible stories, English—
O.T. Genesis. [1. Noah's ark.   2. Noah (Biblical
figure) 3. Bible Stories—O.T.] I. Thomas Nelson
Publishers. II. Series.
BS658.N59   1993
222'.1109505—dc20   93-14131
                                                CIP
                                                AC

93 94 95 96 97—1 2 3 4 5

Printed and bound in the United States of America

NOAH AND THE ARK

In the years after the time of Adam and Eve and their children, the world had become a very bad place where people disobeyed God's laws and did evil things.

In this bad world, there lived a very good man named Noah. He and his family lived a peaceful, quiet life. They obeyed God's laws and loved each other.

God was angry with the people who did not listen to Him. He decided to start over by washing the world clean with a huge Flood. God spoke to Noah and told him that he should save himself and his family by building a large boat, called an Ark.

When Noah and his family
began to work on the Ark,
their neighbors asked them
why they were building a
huge boat so far from the sea.
Noah told them what God had
said, but they laughed at him
and called him crazy. He tried
to get them to change their
ways.

At last, the Ark was finished. God told Noah to load the Ark with enough food for his family and for the animals that would be coming. The first animals to get on the Ark may have been the pet cats and dogs that lived with Noah's family.

The news of the coming Flood spread to the creatures in the nearby woods . . . to the squirrels, the bunnies, the birds, and even old Mr. and Mrs. Mole.

The news was heard by the bears and the deer, the squirrels and the owls in the deep forests. They had to hurry to Noah's Ark.

From the cool, green woods, the news traveled over the rocky deserts. The camels, the buzzards and lizards and even the jackals knew that something important was about to happen.

The news was heard high in the mountains. The goats, the llamas, and the eagles knew they must come to join the other animals on the Ark.

God's message found its way into the thick jungles. The giraffes and the hippos, the tigers and the zebras knew they must hurry to the Ark. The monkeys laughed at the news but they quickly followed the other animals.

The Ark was an amazing sight. Hundreds of animals were streaming to the Ark, two by two. There were lions and tigers and polar bears. There were cows and zebras. There were turtles and turkeys. There were snakes and dragonflies.

Animals were coming from the ends of the Earth. There were bunnies, squirrels, bears, elephants, and kangaroos.

As the last of the animals scampered aboard, Noah noticed the first raindrops of the storm that God had said would bring the great Flood. Soon it would be raining harder than it had ever rained before. Noah and his family entered the Ark and God closed the door.

Suddenly, there was a loud clap of thunder and the rain began to come down very hard. Inside the Ark, everyone was cozy and dry. Even the lions were peaceful for a change, and even the little lambs were not afraid of them.

The wind blew and the rain poured. The Flood came, the waters rose, and soon the Ark was floating free.

It rained for forty days and forty nights. At last, God decided that the Earth had been washed clean. Noah turned to his wife and said, "I think the rain has stopped! Maybe we can land soon."

After many days had passed, Noah decided to send a raven out the window to see if there was a dry place for the bird to land.

The raven just flew around and around, and couldn't find a place to land. The next day Noah sent a dove out to see what she could find. She came back with a green olive branch in her beak. That meant the water had gone down, and somewhere plants were starting to grow again. Noah and his family were overjoyed.

A week later, Noah let the dove go again. This time, the dove didn't return. This meant that the water had gone down and she had found a place to build her nest. The great Flood was over.

Noah and his family praised God and thanked him for keeping them safe. Time passed and the world would soon be filled with people and animals again. Only this time, it was a lot more peaceful.